D1476918

Chris ★ Craft®

AN AMERICAN CLASSIC

Nick Voulgaris III

Foreword by

Ralph Lauren

RIZZOLI
NEW YORK

New York · Paris · London · Milan

CONTENTS

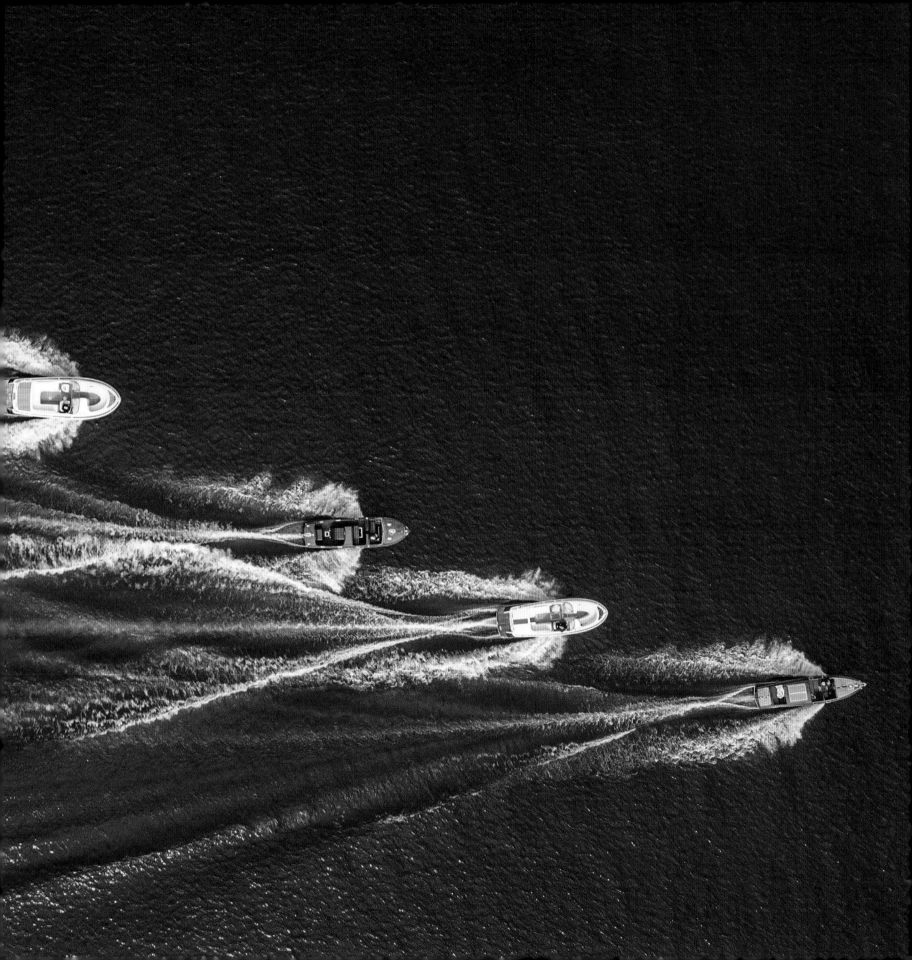

FOREWORD

RALPH LAUREN

I have always loved things that have a timeless beauty to them—a beautiful timepiece, a vintage race car, a weathered barn, a Navaho blanket, an old leather book, and, of course, a handcrafted wooden boat.

I have been inspired over and over again by the romance of the seafaring life, and by so many summers spent with my wife and children in old shingled houses weathered by the salty ocean breezes.

The vessels I have collected were mainly built for the road. Their beauty was often informed by utility. The men who built them would race them competitively so each curve, spoke of a wheel, headlight, and detail was never incidental, but purposely crafted for speed. The founder of Chris-Craft, 13-year-old Christopher Columbus Smith, who built his first wooden boat in 1874, was not seeking that. He simply wanted a boat for cruising the waters of the small town in Michigan where he grew up, but what he built with his hands had the same kind of craftsmanship that I have loved in my cars and eventually inspired those beautiful mahogany runabouts that were steered by the likes of Henry Ford and William Randolph Hearst. Chris-Craft became the iconic brand of American boating. A boat with class and heritage and a timeless spirit.

For 50 years I have been celebrating the heritage of America and the way we live. Many of my advertising campaigns have been situated along the rugged coasts of this land from New England and California to the cold, wide lakes of the Adirondacks. They were always about the stories of families enjoying life, pursuing different pleasures. One I recall in particular shared the beauty of a woman and her young son at the wheel of a vintage mahogany vessel. She steered that boat with amazing confidence, turning it through the waves, creating a wake of whitecaps behind her. It was a very romantic moment, but the boat was as much the heroine as the woman was. Its sleek, dark wood and polished brass with an American flag blowing off the back was breathtaking and authentic. The boat was, of course, a Chris-Craft.

An image from a vintage Ralph Lauren ad campaign aboard a Chris-Craft.

INTRODUCTION

NICK VOULGARIS III

The Chris-Craft brand is one of the most respected and recognized boating names in the world. The company has been building boats of immense beauty for nearly 150 years, ever since company founder Christopher Columbus Smith built his first boat in 1874 in Algonac, Michigan. Its boats are some of the most iconic designs of all time.

Chris-Craft is credited with being one of the driving forces in introducing America to the boating lifestyle. The company and its boats became a cultural phenomenon during the 20th century and quickly grew to become the largest producer of boats in the world. Throughout its storied history, Chris-Craft has built approximately 200,000 boats, and it is estimated the company produced a staggering 800 different models. The company also built components for other famous brands, such as hulls for Garwood and motors for Riva and Hinckley.

This book is the culmination of a lifelong love affair with Chris-Craft that began decades ago, when I was a little boy growing up on Long Island, New York. Although my family always had a sailboat, several family friends had vintage wooden Chris-Craft runabouts that I had the pleasure of riding. I was mesmerized by the gleaming varnished mahogany decks, which had thin white striping applied between each plank. I remember being able to see my reflection in the shiny windshields and polished chrome air vents that were designed to look like small inverted dinghies.

Being aboard those boats when I was young was magical. There was something about the smell of varnish that made the boats feel warm and alive. I remember one particular summer when I was seven or eight years old, spending a lot of time aboard our friend's boat named *Teddy Bear* during a family vacation on Shelter Island, New York. *Teddy Bear* was a 1947 Chris-Craft Utility 22, also known as a Sportsman 22. She was one of the Chris-Crafts built after the war, and she had a white-painted cedar hull because mahogany was scarce. She had a chrome spotlight with a hand control on the dashboard and a vintage fold-down swim ladder. And, as with all her sisterships of that era, she had the throttle control in the center of the steering wheel, which I found fascinating. There was something incredibly freeing about sitting high up on the seat's backrest while getting to steer her and cruise around Dering Harbor (with adult supervision, of course).

When we would go fast on *Teddy Bear*, the forward half of the boat would rise out of the water as if we were about to take off like an airplane—emulating that familiar profile classic runabouts have when speeding along. A few years later, I became enthralled while watching the movie *On Golden Pond*, where a near-identical Sportsman 22 had a starring role alongside Katharine Hepburn and Henry Fonda. There was a scene where their young grandson raced around the lake, sitting high up on the backrest like I had, hands in the air and completely free.

During junior high school, I worked for the owner of *Teddy Bear* on weekends—sanding, scraping, and varnishing the boat. I was determined to learn as much as I could about these classic vessels, and even more determined to one day own one.

I got that chance years later, in 2000, when I stumbled upon a vintage Chris-Craft Lancer 23 that had been sitting in a parking lot for years. She was similar to the Utility 22 in that she had a straight inboard engine, with the motor box in the middle of the boat. She wasn't for sale when I found her, but I reached out to the owner to see if he was willing to part with her. I bought her and spent the next year restoring the boat. I named her *Dasher*, likely a subconscious decision, as the boat would soon deliver that same feeling of being free out on the water that I had experienced as a child. Eighteen years later, *Dasher* still provides my friends and me immense joy out on the water on the east end of Long Island where I keep her.

Today, the name Chris-Craft continues to conjure up visions of sleek runabouts, shiny chrome, and varnished wood. The company continues to thrive, building boats that are a testament to its rich history and American heritage. The boats are evocative and convey a feeling of nostalgia and romance while constantly advancing with both new materials and technology.

In a recent interview, Chris Smith—the 92-year-old grandson of the founder of Chris-Craft—said, "I think the boats that Chris-Craft is building today are great, just great!" It was a clear message and nod that the company is living up to its legendary name.

PAGE 10: A 22-foot Chris-Craft Sportsman in Shelter Island, New York. This model was immortalized in the movie *On Golden Pond* and is credited with the revival of classic runabouts.

OPPOSITE: The author aboard *Dasher*, his classic Chris-Craft, with his dog Charlie.

OVERLEAF: Vintage wooden Chris-Crafts (from left to right): *Saga*, a 1930 38-foot Commuter; *Campaigner*, a 1929 28-foot Runabout; *IV Phunn*, a 1947 22-foot Utility; and *Spirit*, a 1949 19-foot Racing Runabout.

CHAPTER ONE

EARLY HISTORY

The allure of Chris-Craft boats started long before the gleaming mahogany runabouts that made the company famous in the 1920s, and long before the sleek and beautiful speedboats that the company is still building today. • Company founder Christopher Columbus Smith was born in Cottrellville Township, Michigan, on May 20, 1861. Later, his parents moved the family to Algonac, Michigan, the town that would eventually become home to Chris-Craft. • As a young boy, Chris Smith was interested in duck hunting and carved his own decoys out of wood, which likely nurtured his interest in building boats. He built his very first boat, along with his brother, Henry, in 1874. It was a modest 13-foot skiff, but this first experience was the beginning of what became one of the greatest boating empires in the world. • The two brothers went on to build canoes and duckboats and became avid duck hunters and sportsmen. These small boats had no motors and could be rowed or pushed along the seabed with a pole. The resourceful brothers of modest means started a small business of supplying fresh ducks

to local restaurants and markets in Detroit. They also were hired to take people duck hunting on the nearby waterways.

The Smith brothers slowly expanded their boat-building operation; they opened a small boathouse along the waterfront in Algonac and formed the Smith Brothers Boat Builders. They built mostly small rowboats, duckboats, and launches for a local clientele.

In the early 1890s, the brothers began installing steam and naphtha engines in their boats. This was a revolutionary advancement for them, and the small boats were able to cruise along at approximately five miles an hour, a very respectable speed at the time.

Around 1895, Chris purchased a used two-horsepower Stintz gasoline engine that he installed in one of his small launches. The gasoline engine proved to be a more reliable powerplant over the naphtha engines; it could push the small boat to more than eight miles an hour.

Henry ended up being more interested in duck hunting and building a business around that sport, so he left the boatbuilding business. Chris went on as the sole proprietor, and the company's name was formally changed to C. C. Smith, Boat Builder.

Chris Smith continued to grow his fledgling company by building canoes, skiffs, and small runabouts powered by gasoline motors. Of all the different styles of boats that Smith was building, he was most interested in the runabouts. He was interested in racing and was determined to build his boats to move faster and faster. He had a natural eye for hull design. He would first make a small wooden model of the hull, then study and adjust its lines carefully, and finally build the actual full-sized boat.

Smith received his first order for a race boat in 1905. Named *Dart*, and built for Algonac businessman Neil McMillan, the boat could fly across the water at an astounding 25 miles an hour. This was the beginning of what became an illustrious career in building race boats.

As gasoline engines continued to improve and become more reliable, Smith too improved his boats by refining their design, modifying the pitch in their propellers, and shifting the weight—all with the goal of increased speed. Smith even began modifying stock engines and eventually started building his own motors.

Smith received an order for a race boat from Cincinnati businessman John Ryan. Ryan was a wealthy individual who wanted to beat McMillan's *Dart* in races along the St. Clair River and was

PAGE 16: Chris-Craft is known for its use of chrome work and other high-quality materials, as seen here on this vintage runabout. Note the hardware for the louvered windshield and the classic spotlight.

PAGE 19: Four early Chris-Craft Runabouts speed up the St. Clair River in Michigan.

OPPOSITE: The gleaming varnish and chrome on a 1929 28-foot Custom Runabout.

ABOVE: Company founder Christopher Columbus Smith with models aboard a yacht.

willing to spend a lot of money to do so. Smith and Ryan conceived the *Reliance I* and *Reliance II*, which made top speeds of 28 and 31 miles per hour respectively. These speeds may seem insignificant by today's standards, but they were record breaking in the early 1900s.

Ryan had been bitten by the racing bug after several wins, and was also interested in building runabouts for a wider market. In 1910 Smith and Ryan went into business together and formed the Smith-Ryan Boat Company. Ryan's capital infusion allowed the company to not only continue developing its race boats, but also begin building boats for the general public. The new venture offered two standardized runabouts, a 25-foot and 33-foot model. The boats made by the young company were some of the fastest in the world at the time.

Ryan continued to develop his racing program and spent lavishly on his hobby, and since he was an owner of the company he did not have to immediately pay for his boats. Unfortunately, his spending

OPPOSITE: *Rainbow IX*, a very rare 1922 26-foot Chris-Craft Race Boat. Originally named *Packard Chris-Craft II*, she set a world speed record in 1925.

ABOVE: *Miss Detroit*, an early Chris-Craft Race Boat built for speed.

LEFT, TOP: A 1935 ad features a Chris-Craft on top of an automobile.

LEFT, BOTTOM: An early Chris-Craft Runabout with a rare folding convertible top.

OPPOSITE: A Chris-Craft Runabout races down a canal in Miami Beach, Florida, in the 1930s.

OVERLEAF: *Roaring 20s*, a 1929 28-foot triple-cockpit Custom Runabout.

habits and the financial conditions from World War I left him practically bankrupt. His large debts to the Smith-Ryan Company could not be paid, and the two men dissolved their partnership. The company became known as the C. C. Smith Boat & Engine Company.

Not long after, industrialist Garfield "Gar" Wood entered the racing scene by purchasing the *Miss Detroit* syndicate, which was a fast race boat built by Smith. Wood too became intrigued by this sport and also boatbuilding in general. He purchased Smith's company, and Smith and his sons stayed on to manage the business.

The purchase allowed Smith to focus on the design and building of boats and not be burdened with the finances or intricacies of running a growing business. Gar Wood, Chris Smith, and Smith's two sons, Jay and Bernard, entered countless races with boats they had built and consistently broke records. They built boats for a very wealthy clientele, and they traveled the world together setting new records and selling boats.

By the early 1920s, Jay and Bernard Smith convinced their father that it was time to break away from Wood and go back to being a family-run business. There wasn't a specific grievance that they had with Wood, but it is believed the two brothers wanted to make their own mark. The Smith family purchased 20 acres of waterfront land in Algonac, Michigan, and formed the new Chris Smith & Sons Boat Company. Instead of catering to wealthy sportsmen who wanted custom race boats, as was the case in the past, they decided to follow the lead of Henry Ford and build standardized boats for a larger audience at reasonable prices.

The Smiths got a boost to their young business by receiving a contract from Wood to build hulls for his own company. The order for 33-foot "Baby Gar" hulls, as well as repair and modification work to Wood's race boats, allowed the Smiths to hire approximately 30 men for the factory and keep the business running in its early days.

This arrangement worked well for several years, but then it became clear that the orders for Wood, which generated little profit, were an encumbrance to growing Chris Smith's own business. Wood also became frustrated with the relationship, as his own orders were not being given top priority. The two men decided to end their working relationship for good.

The Smiths continued to build their reasonably priced runabouts, and in 1925 produced 111 units in a single year. Jay Smith had

OPPOSITE: A Chris-Craft Cadet comes out of the factory and is loaded on a truck for transport.

ABOVE: Chris-Craft built the hulls for many early Garwood boats.

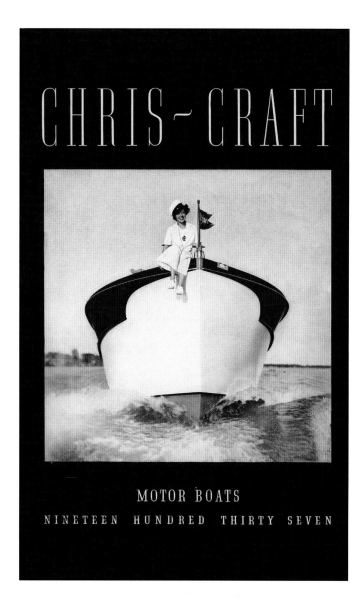

ABOVE: The cover of a 1937 Chris-Craft sales catalog.

OPPOSITE: Images of the original Chris-Craft plant in Algonac, Michigan, during the late 1920s. Chris-Craft was building not only boats, but also its own engines.

the idea to name a special model boat a "Chris-Craft" after his father. Soon after, all boats built by the Chris Smith & Sons Boat Company were known as Chris-Crafts.

The new Chris-Craft boats quickly became popular and the company could not keep up with demand. Smith began to build his boats for the first time with an assembly line, modeled after the automobile industry. This process allowed his skilled craftsmen to focus on one specific task that they could perfect.

In 1926, Chris Smith & Sons began to establish a small dealership network to market and sell the boats, instead of selling directly from the factory to the consumer. The company grew rapidly; by the end of the 1920s, the Smiths were building approximately 1,000 boats per year, which generated more than $3 million in sales.

The boating boom in the United States was in full swing, and Smith believed anyone in the market to purchase an automobile was a potential customer for his boats. To help attract customers, Smith was a pioneer in offering a deferred payment plan, which allowed purchasers to receive delivery on a boat and make payments over 12 months through a local bank he had secured.

The company had become very profitable, in fact making a $300,000 profit in 1929. The factory was now under year-round operation, and yet it still had a backlog of orders. To help streamline components and alleviate some of his production burden, Smith turned to Walter Chrysler of the Chrysler Corporation to provide motors for a portion of his boats. A new Chrysler "Imperial" marine engine was developed for use in Chris-Craft boats. Not only did this arrangement allow the Smiths quick access to engine inventory, but Chrysler also had a global dealer and parts network that was beneficial to Chris-Craft customers. Chrysler was also eager to enter the partnership, as it gave the carmaker access to the burgeoning boating business that he coveted.

Despite the company's focus on building boats designed for the everyday person, interest in the beautiful varnished mahogany Chris-Craft boats began attracting celebrity and wealthy clients. Soon the Astors, Morgans, Vanderbilts, DuPonts, Firestones, and Wrigleys all owned Chris-Craft boats. The company became so well known and valuable that in 1930 an investment firm from New York offered to purchase one-third of the business for $1.125 million through a stock offering. Smith was not initially looking to sell part of the business,

LEFT, TOP: Singer and actress Helen Morgan aboard *Miss Chris-Craft*.

LEFT, BOTTOM: Chris-Craft boats were used as tenders and limousines for many larger yachts. Pictured here is a 1937 16-foot Race Boat.

OPPOSITE: A Chris-Craft showroom in New York City circa 1932 with a 25-foot Custom Runabout in the foreground. Note the Chris-Craft logo on the boat cradles.

but he eventually agreed to the deal and negotiated a nonrefundable $250,000 deposit from the bankers.

As the closing date for the sale approached, the ripple effects from the previous year's stock market crash and the onset of the Great Depression caused the investment firm to default on the purchase. Chris-Craft too began to feel the strains of a crippled economy, and that deposit Smith negotiated is credited with carrying the company for the next several years, saving it from almost certain bankruptcy. Boatbuilders that were not as fortunate to survive the Depression included Sea Lyon, Dodge, Dee Wite, Dart, and others.

To stay lean during the early 1930s, Chris-Craft trimmed its product line and offered stripped-down versions of its runabouts to attract sales. It coined the name "utility" to describe the less-expensive models that lacked many of the luxury features found on its sisterships. The company cut staff and reverted to part-time hours to keep the business afloat. It also introduced a small 15½-foot runabout that was sold for $795 to help attract more entry-level boaters.

Although Chris-Craft operated at a loss for several years as a result of the Depression, the company began to thrive once again by 1936. It soon began to offer "cruisers" with overnight accommodations, and its product range grew. By 1937 the company offered a staggering 97 different models.

The close of the decade came with both joy and sadness. The company was once again on an upswing with strong sales, and Jay Smith had secured the purchase of a 22-acre facility in Holland, Michigan, for additional production space. But Chris Smith, the man responsible for the birth of Chris-Craft, passed away on September 9, 1939, at age 78. Smith had built a legacy that would go on for generations and shape the boating industry for decades to come.

OPPOSITE: An early Chris-Craft Utility, *Shady Lady* is 18 feet long and was built in 1934.

RIGHT, TOP: After the Great Depression, Chris-Craft built models with affordable price tags to help sell boats and keep the factory open.

RIGHT, BOTTOM: In the late 1930s, the company began building larger boats for overnight trips, such as this 1939 36-foot Enclosed Bridge Cruiser.

OVERLEAF: *Saga*, a 1930 38-foot Commuter yacht, in her home waters of Lake Tahoe, Nevada. She is one of only 65 ever built.

OPPOSITE: *Lisa Ann*, a 1930 20-foot Model 100, features a triple-cockpit design.

ABOVE: *Rare Find*, a 1930 20-foot Runabout, and a contemporary 32-foot Launch on Lake Geneva, Wisconsin.

ABOVE: *Sequel*, a 22-foot Chris-Craft Cadet.

OPPOSITE: Detail aboard a 28-foot Custom Runabout with a rare folding top. The convertible's original factory canvas top was supported with steam-bent oak hoops.

OVERLEAF: A picnic lunch is ready aboard *Redhawk*, a 1929 24-foot Model 3. She was ordered new by the U.S. government and used as an undercover patrol boat chasing rumrunners during Prohibition in Chicago (left). The planing hull of a 1939 Custom Runabout. Note the dual chromed air horns and spotlight on the foredeck (right).

OPPOSITE: A 1939 22-foot Utility Sedan.

ABOVE: *Molly-O*, a 1939 25-foot Deluxe Utility, cruises down the bay.

CHAPTER TWO

AMERICA'S BOATBUILDER

C hris-Craft entered the 1940s as the national leader in recreational boating and one of the most well-respected names in the business. The brand also began to have an international presence as its dealership network grew. Chris-Craft boats could be found in dozens of countries around the world. The range of boats being offered was vast, with approximately 100 different models starting with a sporty 15½-foot runabout all the way up to a grand 55-foot motor yacht. • The threat of a world war was eminent, but Chris-Craft still felt strongly about the potential growth of its core business and continued to make expansion plans. The Smith family executed a brilliant deal with the city of Cadillac, Michigan, which allowed Chris-Craft to expand without any hard upfront costs. The company received land and production facilities at no cost from the city in exchange for guaranteeing $250,000 in salaries over several years for local workers. The company then became the outright owner of the land and factory once the salary requirements were met. Chris-Craft also

purchased land in Grand Rapids, Michigan, and Jamestown, New York, for additional facilities.

When the eventual reality of war set in, Chris-Craft was able to use the expanded facilities to win government contracts to build war boats. Its first order was to build engines for 26-foot motor mine yawls in 1941. The motors were used in boats built by the Wheeler Shipyard in Brooklyn, New York, as well as the Southwest Harbor Boat Corporation, also known as Hinckley, in Southwest Harbor, Maine.

Chris-Craft then won a contract to construct more than 1,000 36-foot landing craft vessels that could carry passengers and a vehicle. The boxy boat featured a flat bow panel that lowered down, allowing a Jeep to drive off the boat and onto the shore in shallow water. This contract proved pivotal to Chris-Craft's postwar construction techniques, as it introduced the company to building boats out of plywood and a new sealant called Thiokol.

Government orders for boats continued to dominate the Chris-Craft factories over the next few years. Prior to the war the company had already been crowned as the world's largest builder of boats, yet the new volume of work was so high that the company needed to hire more than 1,000 additional employees.

The construction of civilian boats ceased during the war and did not resume until 1945. Despite not building its civilian boats, Chris-Craft continued to run advertisements in the many periodicals to which it had already made commitments. The ads helped support the war efforts by promoting war bonds for sale, as well as offering hope that recreational boating would eventually return by showcasing future models.

When Japan surrendered in January of 1945, all government military contracts were in effect suspended or canceled, and Chris-Craft returned to the construction of pleasure craft. The company had built more than 10,000 landing craft alone for the war, and it was well positioned—with its strong work force and modern facilities—to lead the boating industry into its return to building boats for recreation.

One of the results of the war that affected the boating industry was an extreme shortage of lumber and other raw materials. The beautiful Philippine mahogany Chris-Craft used on its varnished hulls was in very short supply. This created an enormous problem for Chris-Craft, and other builders as well. The company was forced to

New Chris-Craft 36-ft. Double Stateroom Enclosed Cruiser

And even this picture does not tell the story. For there are 2 complete staterooms forward . . . built-in dinette . . . complete ship's galley . . . you can sleep 6 in solid comfort and cruise where you choose at speeds up to 23 m.p.h. Ready after Victory. See your Chris-Craft Dealer for details. . . . We are 100% on war work now.

Buy U.S. War Bonds Today—
Tomorrow command your own
Chris-Craft

CHRIS-CRAFT CORPORATION, ALGONAC, MICH. ★ WORLD'S LARGEST BUILDERS OF MOTOR BOATS

To appear in full color in:

| Life Magazine | Collier's | Fortune | Esquire | Time | National Geographic |
| Field and Stream | | Outdoor Life | Motor Boating | Yachting | |

PAGE 46: Bow detail on a 1947 Chris-Craft Utility.

PAGE 49: A very rare 18-foot Chris-Craft Utility on Lake Monona, Wisconsin.

OPPOSITE: Three examples of postwar Chris-Crafts during the company's heyday highlight its broad range of models, including a 21-foot Capri, 33-foot Futura, and 55-foot Constellation.

ABOVE: A Chris-Craft ad for U.S. war bonds and the promise for a postwar return to recreational boating. Featured is a 36-foot Enclosed Cruiser.

OPPOSITE: Chris-Craft built more than 10,000 boats for the U.S. government during World War II. Pictured here are four different models.

RIGHT, TOP: A Chris-Craft landing craft with an opening bow allowed troops, gear, and even a Jeep to easily unload on a beach.

RIGHT, BOTTOM: A 42-foot amphibious command boat had machine guns mounted on the fore and aft decks.

OVERLEAF: Four Chris-Craft Barrel Backs ranging from 16 to 19 feet. These models were dubbed "barrel backs" because of the curved barrel-like shape of their sterns.

WORLD'S LARGEST BUILDERS OF MOTOR BOATS

NEW 1959 *Chris★Craft*
SPORTS BOATS · CRUISERS · SPORTS FISHERMEN · MOTOR YACHTS

STANDARD OF VALUE FOR FINE MOTOR BOATS THE WORLD OVER

ABOVE: Chris-Craft dominated the boating market in the 1950s and was the largest boatbuilder in the world: Harsen Smith on the cover of *Time* (left) and the cover of the 1959 Chris-Craft product catalog (right).

OPPOSITE: Chris-Craft introduced boating as a pastime to generations of Americans. Here a 1958 19-foot Cavalier is being launched for a family outing.

trim factory hours and limit the models of boats it offered because it simply could not get deliveries of wood. Finally, the supply of mahogany became so scarce that Chris-Craft switched to cedar wood for its hulls. The cedar was painted white, as it did not look great with stain and varnish. For a period of approximately two years, most Chris-Crafts were white-painted cedar with mahogany trim and accents.

Despite lumber shortages, and at times labor strikes, Chris-Craft was well on its way to becoming the global leader in powerboat production. By the end of the 1940s, the company had become one of the most recognizable brands in the boating industry—so much so that the name "Chris-Craft" became a household term used to describe pleasure craft of any type. Harsen Smith was even featured on the cover of *Time* in 1959.

Chris-Craft's introduction to plywood and Thiokol during World War II was put to good use in the 1950s with the introduction of its Cavalier line of boats built of a five-ply Philippine mahogany

ABOVE: A beautifully restored 1953 35-foot Commander named *Itchin'* moored at Glenthorne Pass, British Columbia.

OPPOSITE: *Bali Hai*, a 1953 24-foot Express Cruiser.

plywood. The Thiokol was used as a sealant and adhesive to bond the pieces together, along with traditional bronze fasteners.

Under the leadership of Jay Smith and his son Harsen, the company began diversifying its product line to include outboard engines, household furniture, and even boat trailers and small motor-home trailers. But its most significant offering of the early 1950s was its new line of kit boats. The Kit Boat Division of the company was created to produce small boat parts that were sold in kit form and assembled by the buyer. This arm of the business quickly became the fastest-growing new product line the company had ever produced.

In the United States the interest in boating was at an all-time high, and the kit boats gave Americans easy access to boat ownership. Magazines such as *Popular Mechanics* and other do-it-yourself publications were in vogue, and Chris-Craft discovered an enormous market for its kits. The kits also gave Chris-Craft access to new markets, as they were sold in department stores, hardware stores, and even purchased by Boy Scouts.

An eight-foot pram rowboat was offered for only $39 and could be assembled in eight to 10 hours. Everything needed to assemble the boat was in the kit, including precut plywood pieces, trim, and hardware, and the shipping crate doubled as a jig frame. Only a few simple household tools were required. Soon Chris-Craft offered dozens of kits ranging all the way up to a 31-foot cruiser. The company advertised an approximate 50 percent savings when buying a boat in kit form versus a turnkey boat that was finished by Chris-Craft.

The company next introduced what became one of its best-selling lines, known as the Sea Skiff. These boats were built in a "lapstrake" style, where each of the planks was overlapped horizontally, and the boats were offered in sizes from 18 to 40 feet. The company also introduced the Constellation series of large motor yachts in the 50-foot range. Chris-Craft pioneered the "flying bridge" on these boats, where the captain could command the boat from an upper deck for optimal visibility. Chris-Craft trademarked the name, and it has since become the standard industry term for a command bridge. Also introduced during the 1950s were the popular Holiday, Continental, Riviera, and Commander models.

In 1955, Chris-Craft purchased the Roamer Boat Corporation, a manufacturer of steel motor cruisers. This allowed Chris-Craft to quickly expand and offer boats built from a material other than

OPPOSITE: Chris-Craft sold nearly 100,000 kit boats through mail order as well as small department and hardware stores, helping the company become a household name during the 1950s and 1960s (clockwise from the top left): a 14-foot Barracuda skiff, a Penguin sailboat, and a Pram before and after assembly.

ABOVE: Chris-Craft also built furniture and small camping trailers, such as this Land Cruiser trailer.

OPPOSITE: A 57-foot 1965 Chris-Craft Roamer, which could be built of steel or aluminum. Chris-Craft acquired the Roamer Boat Corporation in an effort to diversify its wooden boats.

RIGHT, TOP: A 65-foot wooden Motor Yacht toward the end of wooden boat production in 1965.

RIGHT, BOTTOM: Chris-Craft introduced the all-fiberglass 38-foot Commander in 1964.

wood. A new material called fiberglass was also being introduced to the boating industry. Chris-Craft began integrating fiberglass into a few models, including the 21- and 25-foot Cobra, which featured a wooden hull and a fiberglass aft deck with a radical dorsal-style fin. Chris-Craft also developed the Silver Bullet boat, which was built of plywood with fiberglass sheathing.

To quickly expand its capacity to build fiberglass boats, Chris-Craft purchased a small Florida-based manufacturer that built a 15-foot runabout of plywood encased with fiberglass. Unfortunately, the longevity of this boat was not fully proven prior to the purchase. Over time, the plywood separated from the fiberglass and allowed water intrusion, causing the boat to leak. Chris-Craft quickly sold off the Lake 'n Sea Division and became weary of working with fiberglass altogether except in limited applications. This inevitably put Chris-Craft behind the curve during the next decade, as most builders switched to fiberglass construction.

As with the purchase and expansion of its other plants, Chris-Craft negotiated a favorable deal where it purchased a large swath of land in Pompano Beach, Florida, and in turn subdivided parcels it would not need. The proceeds from the subdivision completely financed the construction of the buildings and facilities on the remaining 66 acres of waterfront property.

After calling Algonac, Michigan, home for the better part of a century, Chris-Craft decided to move its main operations to the warm weather of Pompano Beach. The Michigan winters were long and harsh and impeded numerous aspects of the business. The new location allowed for year-round production, in-water testing, and better access to the company's core market along the eastern seaboard.

By the beginning of 1960, Chris-Craft had settled into its new home and was the driving force in recreational boating in the United States and beyond. The company employed nearly 4,000 people and had annual sales in excess of $40 million, with sales in almost every country with access to water. Harsen Smith had no interest in retiring, but soon an opportunity to sell the company came along that he couldn't refuse.

After considerable family debate and reluctant negotiations, Chris-Craft was sold to National Automotive Fibers Inc. (NAFI), which was controlled by New York-based businessman and yacht racer Cornelius Shields. Shields, an avid sailor, soon introduced a line of

ABOVE: A Riva Super Aquarama on Lake Tahoe. Chris-Craft provided motors and other parts to Riva in the 1950s; in fact, the dashboard nameplate on many Rivas were inscribed "Riva Chris-Craft."

OPPOSITE: *007*, a very rare 1955 21-foot Cobra, hull number 7 out of 55 built. She was ordered new by Henry Kaiser and berthed at his Lake Tahoe estate Fleur du Lac (used in the film *The Godfather II*). Coincidentally, the boat's current owner lives there today, and *007* has returned to her original home.

Chris-Craft sailboats to the market, designed by the venerable firm of Sparkman & Stephens. Although Chris-Craft was still producing its line of motorboats in wood, the new line of sailboats was constructed of fiberglass.

With strong sales and a new owner, Chris-Craft soon expanded operations and built factories in Switzerland, Italy, and Canada to fulfill European and North American sales orders. NAFI was keen to capitalize on the name recognition of Chris-Craft, and the NAFI name was changed to Chris-Craft Industries to reflect its ownership of the Chris-Craft brand.

Shields realized Chris-Craft had fallen behind with regards to the evolution of fiberglass. To help alleviate this problem, Chris-Craft purchased boatbuilder Thompson Boats of Cortland, New York, which was known for its fiberglass runabouts with a revolutionary "transdrive" motor later known as the inboard/outboard engine. Chris-Craft enhanced the Thompson boats and launched a new line called Corsair.

Chris-Craft started to convert its other production facilities to fiberglass construction and introduced the all-fiberglass Commander line of boats in 1964. The boats were comfortable motor cruisers and ranged in size from 23 to 60 feet. The 60-foot model was the largest fiberglass production boat built in the world at the time. This new line helped cement Chris-Craft as the dominant builder of fiberglass boats, and soon the entire line of Chris-Craft models were built from this modern, new material.

Under the helm of Cornelius Shields, Chris-Craft built sailboats, such as this 42-foot Comanche built in 1968. The company built more than 700 sailboats from 1965 to 1976, with many of them designed by Sparkman & Stephens.

ABOVE: A 25-foot Sportsman and 1956 26-foot Continental cruise in Lake Geneva, Wisconsin.

OPPOSITE: A 17-foot Chris-Craft Utility cruises off the New York Yacht Club in Newport, Rhode Island.

OPPOSITE: Dashboard detail of a 1947 17-foot Chris-Craft Deluxe Runabout. Chris Smith was a fan of the gauges made by Stewart Warner and used them on the majority of his boats. They were customized with the Chris-Craft logo.

ABOVE: A 1947 17-foot Deluxe Runabout on a still lake at dawn. This was a very popular boat, and nearly 2,000 units were built from 1946 to 1950.

OVERLEAF: *Wecatchem*, a 1948 25-foot Sportsman with a bimini top.

ABOVE: *Double Barrel*, a 1939 19-foot Custom Runabout.

OPPOSITE: Bow hardware on a 1940 Chris-Craft Barrel Back.

OVERLEAF: *Black Beauty*, a 1957 33-foot Futura in exquisite condition. She is believed to be the only Futura ever delivered with a black hull (left). Chris-Crafts often stay in the same family for generations; there are four generations cruising aboard *Black Beauty* in this photograph (right).

OPPOSITE: A 1955 22-foot Chris-Craft Continental, one of 20 boats in the series that came with factory hardtops.

RIGHT, TOP AND BOTTOM: Two examples of a 26-foot Continental.

OVERLEAF: This 1948 20-foot Custom Runabout features a rare fold-down windshield.

OPPOSITE: *Marianne*, a 1960 50-foot Constellation motor cruiser. Although painted white, she was built with a solid mahogany planked hull. She is one of only 42 built.

ABOVE: *Baby Grand*, a 1954 28-foot Semi-Enclosed Cruiser.

ABOVE: Two Chris-Craft 22-foot Sportsmans. The white one on the left is named *Joltin' Joe* and was owned by baseball legend Joe DiMaggio.

OPPOSITE: *Tango*, a 27-foot Semi-Enclosed model on Lake Tahoe, Nevada.

OPPOSITE: A 22-foot Chris-Craft Holiday. Note the trademark Chris-Craft vents on the foredeck that resemble inverted dinghies.

RIGHT, TOP: *Deadman's Curve*, a classic Chris-Craft Holiday. The Holiday models were built with the same hull as the Continental, but had a utilitarian interior at a more attractive price.

RIGHT, BOTTOM: *Fish Tales*, a mahogany Holiday finished with blond trim.

OVERLEAF: *Eulipion*, a 1947 Express Cruiser. She is one of only 302 that were built from 1946 to 1948.

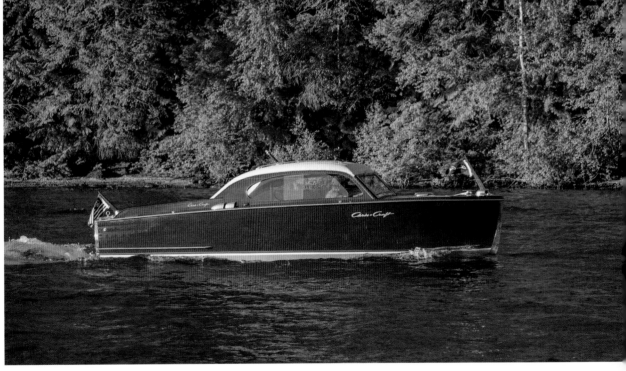

OPPOSITE: A Chris-Craft Sportsman cruises on Lake Tahoe, Nevada. This boat was one of Chris-Craft's most popular models, with sizes ranging from 15 feet to more than 30 feet long.

RIGHT, TOP: *Heavenly Days*, a 1948 25-foot Sportsman. Note the centerline walkthrough, as she is equipped with twin Chris-Craft engines.

RIGHT, BOTTOM: *Pondzi Scene*, a 1949 22-foot Utility Sedan, which features the factory hardtop.

OVERLEAF: A rare 19-foot Silver Arrow that was built of wood with a fiberglass skin. This was one of the earliest models where Chris-Craft began working with fiberglass. She is one of only 92 ever built.

ABOVE AND OPPOSITE: *Mister President* and *West Winds*, two nearly identical 1947 25-foot Sportsmans on Lake Tahoe. These comfortable runabouts can easily accommodate seven people.

OVERLEAF: *Baby Skip*, a 1953 19-foot Racing Runabout powered by a 240-horsepower Ford engine.

ABOVE: A 1962 28-foot Constellation cruises on the Niagara River in northern New York.

OPPOSITE: *Knotty '48* is a 1948 17-foot Deluxe Runabout powered by her original 90-horsepower Chris-Craft engine.

OVERLEAF: In 1961, Chris-Craft built a special run of 11 21-foot Continental models with a landau top with opening hatches, such as *Fin & Tonic* pictured here (left). *Twin Finn* is a 1959 21-foot Continental. She is built of mahogany with fiberglass fins and other details modeled after the automobile industry at the time (right).

ABOVE: A 57-foot Constellation built of mahogany alongside a contemporary 29-foot Catalina built of fiberglass. The 57-foot Constellation model was one of the last wooden Chris-Crafts to be built.

OPPOSITE: An early 1960s 23-foot Chris-Craft Sea Skiff in Shelter Island, New York.

CHAPTER THREE

FIBERGLASS REVOLUTION

The introduction of fiberglass had a profound effect on the boating industry, and the art of traditional wooden boat construction was eventually abandoned in light of this new material. Fiberglass boats were easier to build and easier to maintain, and the hulls and decks did not expand or contract like their wooden predecessors. The hulls did not require soaking, caulking, or constant paint and varnish. And although it took some time for both the industry and consumers to buy into fiberglass, it eventually became the predominant material of boatbuilding. • Chris-Craft had experimented with fiberglass in the 1950s with its Silver Arrow boat, as well as with the purchase of the Lake 'n Sea boat company. Both of these ventures involved layering fiberglass over a traditional planked or plywood hull. At the time, Chris-Craft was skeptical of fiberglass and eventually abandoned working with the new material, instead focusing on wooden boatbuilding. After all, Chris-Craft was the largest builder of wooden boats then; it had millions of dollars invested in tooling, jigs, and

patterns for its wooden boats. It also had thousands of employees who had spent years training and learning how to perfect wooden boatbuilding. Pivoting to fiberglass was an enormous challenge, and the company resisted for as long as possible.

Fiberglass was relatively inexpensive. It became easier to build boats, and the cost of entry into the marketplace decreased substantially for new boatbuilders. Dozens of small boat manufacturers began to pop up in the 1960s, becoming new competitors. Prior to the advent of fiberglass, there were only a handful of boatbuilders that could be considered competition for Chris-Craft.

By the mid-1960s, it became clear to the company's management that it needed to make the change to fiberglass. In 1964, Chris-Craft introduced its new line of all-fiberglass Commander boats, which were an immediate success. Soon the Sea Skiff line and all other models were built of fiberglass as well. Chris-Craft's last wooden boat was a 57-foot mahogany Constellation that was built in 1972.

With new ownership, new materials, and new construction methods, it was certainly a time for change at Chris-Craft. The company was able to embrace this change and still maintain its top place in the boating world. Herbert Siegel organized a takeover of Chris-Craft Industries in 1968 and become chairman of the board and president. Siegel, a shrewd businessman, had vast experience in manufacturing, aviation, broadcasting, and television businesses. Siegel intended to leverage the Boat Division's recognizable name and profitability, and diversify Chris-Craft Industries to become the dominant leader in the recreational and leisure businesses. Chris-Craft Industries was now composed of the Boating Division, Television and Broadcasting Division, and Industrial Division.

To further strengthen Chris-Craft's offerings of fiberglass boats, the company introduced the sporty Lancer line of runabouts, which were available in full inboard or inboard/outboard motor configurations. These popular boats ranged from 17 to 25 feet. The Lancer became one of the company's most iconic designs, and it is still revered today. In Sweden, for instance, there is a large owners' club with a cultlike following devoted to this particular model.

The company also introduced the fiberglass Catalina line of boats to appeal to larger families who wanted the ability to take overnight trips. These roomy cruisers ranged from 25 to 50 feet and offered comfortable sleeping accommodations, heads (bathrooms),

PAGE 104: A custom stainless-steel windshield frame on a contemporary Chris-Craft.

PAGE 107: A 1969 19-foot Chris-Craft Commander Super Sport. This was one of the company's first boats to be constructed entirely from fiberglass.

OPPOSITE: A 42-foot Chris-Craft Sport Fisherman in Block Island, Rhode Island. This model was often equipped with outriggers for offshore fishing.

ABOVE: A 24-foot Sea Skiff Ranger built in 1965. This popular line of boats was built of lapstrake plywood before the company switched to fiberglass.

ABOVE: A 17-foot Chris-Craft Corsair Sport-V, powered by a "transdrive" inboard/outboard motor. Chris-Craft acquired the tooling to this fiberglass boat, as well as the engine technology, when it purchased the Thompson Boat Company in 1962.

OPPOSITE: A 46-foot Chris-Craft Constellation. This model featured three sleeping cabins.

OVERLEAF: *Wood Island* is a 19-foot Commander Super Sport, later to be called the XK-19 with slight modifications.

full galleys, and showers. With its clean, modern lines, the Catalina soon became a popular model for the growing segment of families who wanted to spend time on the water.

Despite the success of the newer fiberglass Chris-Craft models, the boating industry as a whole experienced a decline in sales by the end of the 1970s. To adjust, Chris-Craft tightened its belt by limiting production schedules and the number of models offered, similar to what was done during the Great Depression and after each war. But after a few years of not showing signs of a rebound, Chris-Craft Industries—which was now a publicly traded company—decided to sell off the coveted Boat Division and focus on its other core businesses.

Since the parent company, previously called National Automotive Fibers Inc. (NAFI), was now publicly known and traded as Chris-Craft Industries, the board decided to sell the Boat Division but retain ownership of the name. A small group of investors led by Dale Murray and his company Murray Industries purchased the Boat Division, which was renamed Murray Chris-Craft. As part of the deal, Murray entered into an agreement to license the Chris-Craft name from Chris-Craft Industries. Murray was able to attract a celebrity list of investors and advisors, including F. Lee Bailey, television's Ed McMahon, and General Alexander Haig.

Under Murray's leadership, Chris-Craft quickly regained market share and by 1986 annual sales hit an all-time high of $175 million annually. To keep up with production demand, the company purchased Uniflite Inc. for expanded manufacturing facilities and the molds to Uniflite's fleet of larger boats. Murray, along with other partners, also purchased the fabled Donzi Marine. Murray continued to foster the existing lines of boats and also introduced the Sea Hawk line of fishing boats and Amerosport cruisers. The company also introduced the sporty Scorpion and Stinger high-performance "cigarette-style" boats. The 39-foot Stinger was a focal point in season one of television's *Miami Vice*.

By the late 1980s, there was an overall consolidation happening in the marine industry. A few key players were acquiring many of the newer fiberglass boatbuilding companies that had emerged in the previous two decades. Outboard Marine Company (OMC), which owned Johnson and Evinrude Outboards, had purchased nearly 20 different brands of powerboat companies. Brunswick, the parent of Mercury Marine, had purchased Bayliner and Sea Ray Boats and

OPPOSITE: *Dasher*, the author's 23-foot Chris-Craft Lancer, in Sag Harbor, New York. This was the first runabout that Chris-Craft did not design in-house. The design was conceived by racing legend Jim Wynne, who also invented the first sterndrive, which was licensed to Volvo Penta.

RIGHT, TOP: A 1986 26-foot Chris-Craft Stinger. A larger sistership, the 38-foot Stinger, was featured on the television show *Miami Vice*.

RIGHT, BOTTOM: A 1988 Scorpion, a product of the company's focus on fast sport boats during the 1980s.

suddenly became the leader in the industry. Both conglomerates were now serious competition for Chris-Craft.

To bolster the company's finances to compete with the many new brands, and also to cover substantial losses from a failed real estate venture, Murray sought outside capital. In 1987, he partnered with a Saudi investment firm. Unfortunately, Murray gave up his majority control in the transaction and was pushed out of the company when the magnitude of his real estate losses became evident.

The company was forced into bankruptcy shortly thereafter, and in 1989 industry titans Genmar (led by Irwin Jacobs) and OMC bid against each other to become the new owner of the venerable Chris Craft company. OMC prevailed with the winning bid, and once again a separate licensing deal was struck with Chris-Craft Industries for use of the name.

A double-cabin Chris-Craft 422 Catalina
in Block Island, Rhode Island.

LEFT, TOP: The sporty Chris-Craft XK-19 on Lake Michigan. Only 275 of these boats were built from 1950 to 1975.

LEFT, BOTTOM: One of the last Chris-Craft Cavalier models built of plywood before the company switched to fiberglass.

OPPOSITE: A 35-foot Chris-Craft Commander, the model that catapulted the company into being one of the top builders of fiberglass boats during the 1960s and 1970s.

OVERLEAF: A rare Chris-Craft XK-18 model. Only 201 boats were built from 1971 to 1973, and they featured a revolutionary jet engine with no propeller. Also pictured in the background is a 19-foot Commander Super Sport.

OPPOSITE: *Barbara Ann*, a 1985 Chris-Craft 422 Sport Fisherman at anchor in Madisonville, Louisiana.

OVERLEAF: A 1963 31-foot Chris-Craft Sea Skiff, *Mona Monique*, on Lake Tahoe. As with many Chris-Crafts, she was bought new and has been in the same family for several generations. She was one of the company's wooden holdovers before all boats were built out of fiberglass (left). *Frilla*, an early fiberglass Chris-Craft Catalina, in Sag Harbor, New York (right).

A Chris-Craft 55-foot
Commander Flush Deck
moored in North Haven,
New York. This boat features
the optional command
bridge steering station.

OPPOSITE: *A/Sea Craft*, a 1982 36-foot Commander Tournament Fisherman, on the east end of Long Island, New York.

ABOVE: A popular cruising vessel, the 41-foot Chris-Craft Flush Deck—seen here in Block Island, Rhode Island—
has fore and aft sleeping cabins, two heads, an ample galley, and a spacious salon.

CHAPTER FOUR

REINVENTING A CLASSIC

From approximately 1989 to 2000, Chris-Craft was under the ownership of Outboard Marine Company (OMC) and struggling to maintain market share. OMC was a large conglomerate, which included Johnson and Evinrude outboard engines and six boat companies. However, under OMC's leadership, the iconic Chris-Craft brand seemed to have lost its way. • OMC was having its own difficulties, as it became overleveraged at the same time that its core businesses were shrinking. There was an attempt to save the business in 1997 by a group of investors led by George Soros (and Carl Icahn), who took the company private. Those efforts unfortunately could not revive OMC, and in 2000 the company filed for Chapter 11 bankruptcy protection. • Enter business partners Stephen Julius and Steve Heese, two entrepreneurs who met each other at Harvard Business School during the 1980s and eventually were responsible for saving Chris-Craft through their investment company, Stellican Ltd. The two men had many things in common,

PAGE 130: Interior detail of a vintage Chris-Craft Runabout. Note the chrome trim and the throttle control lever at the center of the steering wheel.

PAGE 133: The impressive hull shape of a Chris-Craft Launch with its deep-V design and flared bow. This now-iconic model was introduced in 2001 as part of the company's return to classic styling.

ABOVE: Chris-Craft uses an abundance of teak on the closed-deck Corsair line.

OPPOSITE: Three modern classics off the coast of Florida (from left to right): a Silver Bullet 20, a Corsair 27, and a Corsair 34.

OVERLEAF: The Chris-Craft Launch 34 features an open-bow seating area. The ample beam provides stability at sea and seating for 12 people.

especially their passion for heritage brands and building beautiful objects. Julius was not a stranger to turnarounds of iconic brands and had previously purchased, rebuilt, and successfully sold the legendary Italian boatbuilder Riva. Like Chris-Craft, Riva had immense heritage, but had also lost its way and suffered from an inflexible, inefficient, and costly labor force; insufficient distribution channels; and a limited product range. Heese had considerable experience in global business operations and was adept at identifying inefficiencies within the companies he rebuilt.

The two partners became very interested in the opportunity to purchase Chris-Craft when it was announced it would be auctioned. There were obstacles, however. First, there was fierce competition to buy the company's assets, as Chris-Craft was and is arguably the

most iconic and recognized boating brand in the world. The second issue was that only the boatbuilding assets, including the factory, tooling, and inventory—all located in Sarasota, Florida—were for sale. The name "Chris-Craft" was still owned separately by a quite distinct publicly listed company called Chris-Craft Industries, and the Chris-Craft brand was not available for sale.

Julius and Heese were not really interested in buying the boatbuilding assets without also owning the name. They reached out to Herbert Siegel, chairman of Chris-Craft Industries, who had owned the rights to the name since the 1960s and licensed it to the factory building the boats. Siegel collected a handsome royalty each year for the use of the name and was firm in his refusal to sell the famous brand. But as the auction approached, Julius learned that Rupert Murdoch's News Corporation was acquiring Chris-Craft Industries. Murdoch was purchasing Siegel's company for its string of cable networks, and the Chris-Craft name was part of that purchase. Julius leaped into action and negotiated directly with News Corp., laying the groundwork to purchase an option on the Chris-Craft trademark if the deal in fact happened.

Despite not being able to purchase the trademark rights to Chris-Craft prior to the auction, Julius still attended for OMC's assets in March 2001. In the first round of the auction, Stellican's bid to purchase the Chris-Craft boatbuilding arm on its own was initially successful. However, when all of OMC's assets (including the outboard engine division and six other boat brands) were put up for sale as one lot, Genmar Industries emerged as the successful winner. Irwin Jacobs of Genmar had partnered with Bombardier to make the purchase. Jacobs had unsuccessfully bid on Chris-Craft a decade earlier and was determined to prevail in the auction this time around. Julius, frustrated by the loss, told Jacobs to call him if he ever wanted to sell the Chris-Craft part of the business.

A few days later, Julius got that very call. Jacobs had decided he did not want to spend the time or investment on turning Chris-Craft around, especially without owning the rights to the legendary name. Jacobs, unaware that Julius had an option on the name, was instead going to focus on the other assets that were acquired from the OMC auction.

Through persistence and perhaps a bit of luck, on the same day in late March 2001 Stellican simultaneously closed on the purchase

of the Chris-Craft factory and assets and the deal that secured its option to purchase the Chris-Craft name from News Corp. Julius and Heese were still taking a bit of a gamble that the News Corp. acquisition of Chris-Craft Industries would close, and they would end up in possession of both the trademark rights and the factory. If the deal fell through, they would end up with only the boatbuilding facility and not control of the Chris-Craft name.

But by August of that same year, the News Corp. deal in fact closed, and Stellican exercised its option to purchase the Chris-Craft name. This was the first time in approximately 40 years that the name "Chris-Craft" was reunited with the factory that was building its famous boats.

Now that Julius and Heese—together with a minority investor, Clayton McNeel—were in possession of both the factory and the prestigious Chris-Craft brand and trademarks, they set out on the arduous journey of restoring the prominence of one of the most coveted names in boating history. Their goal was to create boats that met the promise the Chris-Craft brand conveyed. Simply put, Julius

OPPOSITE: This bow detail on a Chris-Craft Launch highlights the custom-designed bow light and pop-up cleat.

ABOVE, LEFT: Chris-Craft manufactures all of its upholstered components to ensure top-quality products.

ABOVE, RIGHT: Chris-Craft remains true to its roots with its use of teak accents and flooring.

OVERLEAF: Stern view of a Chris-Craft Capri with aft lounging pad.

and Heese wanted to create the highest-quality boat that would be worthy of the nameplate that adorned it. They knew the existing product line of boats had to be abandoned, and they began to develop a new line that would possess the qualities of earlier Chris-Crafts. A tremendous investment had to be made in developing the new designs, tooling, and molds to make the conceptual boats a reality. Although continuing down the path with the company's existing boats would have been the easier and less expensive option, the partners acknowledged the awesome responsibility they had as stewards and caretakers of the world's most famous boating brand.

Julius had a similar experience when he owned Riva, where he focused on the company's heritage and departed from its existing models to design a new Aquariva 33. The boat was a huge success, as it emulated the romance and soul of the older Rivas, especially the Aquarama Special. Julius and Heese knew if they were to be successful with Chris-Craft, they too needed to build boats that had the DNA expected from the company's heritage of classically styled runabouts. The men scoured company archives for inspiration for the new boats they would eventually build. New hull shapes were conceived with sweeping lines, flared bows, and gentle tumble-home transoms that evoked the passion and heritage aligned with the company's roots.

Chris-Craft introduced several new runabouts in its first few years of production, including the now-iconic Launch, Corsair, and Roamer models. The boats immediately stood out in a sea of average-looking competitors with their classic styling and drop-dead gorgeous looks. An abundance of the best materials—such as teak, polished chrome, and stainless steel—were used on each model. Hand-stitched upholstery made in-house was carefully crafted one boat at a time, and custom windshields graced each model. The new line of Chris-Crafts immediately made waves with buyers, and the boating industry took notice. Sales of the new boats soared, and the company was well on its way to once again being one of the world's most iconic brands.

The company saw the need in the marketplace for other models with varying functions, but that would still carry the lines and style of the reborn Chris-Craft boats. It introduced the Catalina line of center-console boats, which were conceived as a "gentleman's" utility boat. The boats serve as a great platform for offshore cruising and fishing. Powered by outboard motors, the boats are incredibly

versatile, nimble, and fast. Next, Chris-Craft introduced the Calypso line of dual-console runabouts designed for family excursions and day trips. Powered by outboard motors as well, the boats are great performers and favorites for waterskiing and wakeboarding. The larger versions of both models even feature small bathrooms, or heads, as they are properly called.

More recently the company introduced the classically styled Carina and Capri lines, which feature plumb bows that are finished with chrome cutwaters along the forward edge of the hull. This unique design feature was found on the iconic Chris-Crafts of the 1920s and 1930s.

Julius and Heese are perfectionists when it comes to building their boats, and that is certainly evident with what is coming out of their factory. For instance, the legendary shine on their boats is due to a labor-intensive, multi-stage paint process in the company's high-tech spray booth. The process includes applying two coats of sealer over the gel coat, then two coats of the desired color, and then three coats of clear. And as if that was not enough, the hulls are then sanded first with 1500-grit sandpaper, then 2000-grit, then 3000-grit, and finally 5000-grit. Last, the craftsmen apply a rubbing compound and final sealer wax to ensure the most perfect gleam.

The finished products are truly breathtaking and undeniably Chris-Crafts. The boats are adorned with an abundance of deck hardware like their famous predecessors, including polished trumpet horns, custom cleats, vintage-styled running lights, flagpoles, and teak accents.

"We are in the business of creating art, and that art just happens to be boats," Julius once explained in an interview, and he is correct. The boats Chris-Craft is building today are truly works of art that reflect the brand's rich heritage and celebrated past.

OPPOSITE: Chris-Craft has always been famous for the styling of its dashboards and instruments, as seen here on a Corsair model.

OVERLEAF: A Corsair 30 cruises off of Sarasota, Florida. The large stern platform provides ample space for lounging and recreation.

PAGE 146: A Catalina 30 Pilothouse with a fixed windscreen and hardtop. Note the hull-side door for easy entry.

PAGE 147: Chris-Craft engineers designed a roomy cabin space under the console and foredeck of the Catalina 30.

OPPOSITE: The comfortable aft deck of a Roamer 43.

OVERLEAF: Sharp and classic styling aboard a Capri 21 with custom hull paint (left). Instrument detail on a Capri 21. The Chris-Craft logo has been found on the company's gauges since the 1920s (right).

OPPOSITE: A Corsair 30 zips through the warm waters off Florida's coast. Note the ample seating in the cockpit and trademark trumpet horns.

OVERLEAF: The Chris-Craft Calypso, an open-bow runabout powered by outboards, is well suited for family cruising and water sports. This Calypso 30 features a factory hardtop and twin outboard motors.

ABOVE: The well-appointed interior of the Corsair 34 features a head, small galley, and sleeping accommodations for two people.

OPPOSITE: Generous use of teak and polished stainless steel give the graceful design of the Corsair 34 a classic feel true to Chris-Craft's heritage.

OVERLEAF: A Carina 21 with open-bow seating. Note the stainless-steel cutwater and plumb bow, a design cue adopted from Chris-Craft runabouts built more than 100 years ago.

OPPOSITE: A white Chris-Craft Carina 21 out cruising.

ABOVE: Attention to detail and the company's heritage styling is evident with the teak decking on the bow of this Chris-Craft Corsair.

ABOVE: Custom paintwork, teak, and polished metals are all elements that go into building a Chris-Craft, perpetuating the brand's legacy.

OPPOSITE: A Chris-Craft Launch 27 heads out of the marina. The functional design of the dual bucket seats with stainless-steel grab rails is exclusive to Chris-Craft. The upholstery is hand stitched at the company's factory in Sarasota, Florida.

OPPOSITE: The graceful lines of a Capri 27. This model was designed with a low transom, making getting in and out of the water easier. A cushion fits over the aft teak deck for sunbathing when desired.

OVERLEAF: The roomy interior of the Launch 38 features two double bunks, a galley, and a head. The interior is finished with fine wood trim and plenty of light from overhead hatches (left). A bird's-eye view of this Launch 38 reveals the thoughtful deck layout, with numerous seats and lounging areas and plenty of room for recreation and entertaining. The cabinet behind the helm seat contains an outdoor cooking space with a sink, refrigerator, and icemaker (right).

CHAPTER FIVE

CHRIS-CRAFT TODAY

There are few boating brands that have had the success and longevity of Chris-Craft. During the 19th and 20th century, the company permeated American culture and introduced generations of people to boating. Chris-Craft went on to become the global leader in powerboating with its runabouts and cruisers being sold around the world. The brand is synonymous with life on the water, so much so that in some foreign languages the name "Chris-Craft" translates to "small runabout." • Chris-Craft boats have been immortalized in such movies as *On Golden Pond* and *Mission Impossible 3* and such television shows as *Miami Vice*. The boats have graced advertising campaigns for companies such as Ralph Lauren and others that wish to convey the message of true American heritage and classic design. • The boats the company is building today are undeniably Chris-Craft, with a modern take on a truly classic runabout. Whether it's the throaty rumble of the exhaust or the extensive use of teak and polished metals, the boats possess the same style and elegance of their predecessors built more than a century ago. I believe company founder Christopher Columbus Smith would be very pleased indeed.

PAGE 168: Stephen Julius and Steve Heese, the two men responsible for Chris-Craft's turnaround over the past two decades, are passionate about creating beautiful boats with an abundance of "deck jewelry," as they call it. Here dual trumpet horns adorn the deck of a Corsair model.

PAGE 171: A silhouette of a Launch 27. Chris-Craft designed a modern adaptation of its classic bow light and flagpole base after careful study of the company's archives. The polished stainless-steel anchor roller is integral to the hull and makes the arduous task of anchoring a breeze with the push of a button.

PAGES 172–173: A modern Carina 21 paired with her vintage sistership. The Carina embraces numerous design elements of her predecessor, including a plumb bow, stainless-steel cutwater, and gentle tumble-home transom.

OPPOSITE: The deep-V of the Launch 27 is designed to deliver a superior ride even in rough seas. The flared bow deflects waves and spray and keeps occupants dry.

OVERLEAF: A Corsair 30 and Capri 21 go through the paces near the company's Florida headquarters.

PAGE 178: A Catalina 26 heads out to sea on a fishing expedition.

PAGE 179: A flag-blue Catalina 26 at anchor. A hatch on the forward end of the steering station reveals a small bathroom.

OPPOSITE: One of the many unique metallic paint colors available, seen here on a Launch 34.

OVERLEAF: The next generation of sailors help maintain their Chris-Craft. It is not uncommon to find Chris-Crafts owned by the same family for multiple generations.

OPPOSITE: The family-friendly Calypso 30 is equipped with a factory hardtop and side door on the hull.
Note the telescoping bimini on the aft end of the hardtop for additional protection from the sun and rain.

ABOVE: Children leap into Lake Geneva near Big Foot Beach, Wisconsin.

ABOVE: The well-laid-out helm station of a Launch 28 has all the controls within easy reach.

OPPOSITE: All of the stitching on the upholstery is done in-house at Chris-Craft. Pictured here is the Launch 30. The teak step lifts up and converts into a cocktail table.

OVERLEAF: A fleet of vintage mahogany Chris-Crafts speed along with two Launches.

ABOVE: There is no mistaking the classic lines of Chris-Craft. Here a Launch 27 rests near a sandy beach.

OPPOSITE: A Corsair 27 enters Sag Harbor, New York.

OVERLEAF: Three classic Chris-Crafts run on Lake Geneva, Wisconsin. The company's thoughtful cockpit design and generous accommodations continue today (left). A Corsair 27 on a bank turn. The hull strakes incorporated into the design of each Chris-Craft provide superior tracking and stability (right).

OPPOSITE: The teak workmanship on a Corsair 30. Note the opening cabin hatch and fixed roof lights, which provide a bright and well-lit interior cabin.

OVERLEAF: A Chris-Craft Catalina 29 at anchor off of Aegina Island, Greece (left). Kids play on the swim platform of a Corsair 30 (right).

OPPOSITE: A Chris-Craft Speedster 20 in Sarasota, Florida.

OVERLEAF: A Chris-Craft Launch 27 anchored during the summer months in Lake Tahoe, Nevada (left). Charlie the Labradoodle on a Launch 27 in Sag Harbor, New York (right).

OPPOSITE: Kids and a yellow Labrador have fun on a Chris-Craft Launch.

OVERLEAF: The elegant lines of the Chris-Craft Corsair 36. The hardtop and large glass windows provide protection from the elements and superior visibility.

OPPOSITE: The opening hull door aboard the Calypso 30 is great for swimming or hauling in big game fish.

ABOVE: *Neptune*, a Capri 21, is quite at home alongside a large yacht off Sunset Beach in Shelter Island, New York.

ABOVE: The bow of a Chris-Craft Launch.

OPPOSITE: The gleaming hull of a Corsair 30. The company's proprietary paint process involves seven coats to achieve this most spectacular shine.

OPPOSITE: The bow of a Catalina near the Sakonnet Light in Little Compton, Rhode Island.

OVERLEAF: A Corsair 27 and vintage Continental off Gage Marine in Wisconsin. This location on Lake Geneva has been a Chris-Craft dealer since the 1920s.

OPPOSITE: A Corsair 25 at sunset in the Venetian Islands of Miami, Florida.

OVERLEAF: An American brand since 1874, Chris-Craft continues to build boats that pay tribute to the company's celebrated heritage. Pictured here is the Carina 21.

OPPOSITE: Chris-Craft's owners, Stephen Julius and Steve Heese, aboard a Corsair 30. The two partners are responsible for the brand's return to prominence.

ABOVE: Proudly made in the United States, Chris-Craft employs approximately 300 craftspeople in its Sarasota, Florida, facility.

ACKNOWLEDGMENTS

Having the chance to write a book on Chris-Craft has truly been an honor and privilege. I have been an admirer of the brand ever since I first stepped aboard a 1947 22-foot Utility as a young boy on Long Island, New York.

I'd like to thank the current owners of Chris-Craft—Stephen Julius and Steve Heese—for entrusting me to tell the story of the venerable brand they have painstakingly resurrected over the past two decades. They have worked tirelessly to create a modern boat that evokes the romance and passion Chris-Craft is known for. I'd also like to thank Allison Scharnow and Jennifer Tee at Chris-Craft for their input and for being such a vital part of the book.

I would like to thank my publishers, Charles Miers and James Muschett at Rizzoli, for once again giving me the incredible opportunity to write a book with this iconic publishing house. I am grateful for this continued creative partnership.

I would like to thank my editor at Rizzoli, Candice Fehrman, whose finesse and style always complement my words. I would like to acknowledge Pam Sommers and Jessica Napp for the enormous amount of work they do in promoting these projects. Thank you to designer Susi Oberhelman for her incredible eye in the design of this book and its cover. Also thank you to my literary agent Carla Glasser, whose continued cheerleading keeps me signing up for more books.

I'd like to thank Mr. Ralph Lauren for writing the foreword to this book and sharing his creative insight. I have been a fan of his classic style since I was a young boy, and I would mow lawns to earn money so I could buy Polo shirts at age 12. His brand and vision are perfect complements to the work of Chris-Craft, and it is an honor to have him lend his name and words to this book. I would also like to thank Alfredo Paredes and Mary Randolph Carter at the Ralph Lauren Corporation for all of their help in putting this book together.

A special thanks to Patti Hinson and Brock Switzer at the Mariners' Museum in Virginia for their invaluable help in producing this book. The Mariners' Museum houses the vast Chris-Craft archive that contains countless images, line drawings, and other historical documents. The museum is highly recommended for those having a keen interest in maritime history.

I am grateful to Sierra Boat Works, Gage Marine, the Antique and Classic Boat Society, the Chris-Craft Antique Boat Club, the Chris-Craft Commander Club, and Woodyboater.com for all of their participation with this project and for helping source images and data. Also thank you to all of the photographers and boat owners who participated in this book, whose passion for classic boats and Chris-Craft continues to give the company worldwide prominence.

Last, I would like to acknowledge the founder of Chris-Craft, Christopher Columbus Smith, as well as his family and the many craftsmen who have built an enduring legacy of beautiful boats that has lasted more than 144 years.

The author, Nick Voulgaris, and his dog, Charlie, aboard his vintage Chris-Craft *Dasher* off Shelter Island, New York.

PHOTOGRAPHY CREDITS

© Mayra Alvarez: p. 38.

© Billy Black: pp. 88 and 89.

© Antoine Boon: pp. 136–137.

© Indi Boon: p. 197.

© Sarah Bridgeman: p. 98.

© Clyde Byers: p. 115 (bottom).

Courtesy of Chris-Craft: pp. 21, 104, 138, 139 (both), 140–141, 147 (both), 151, 156, 168, 171, 186, 187, 194–195, and back cover.

© Clint Clemens: pp. 1, 130, 133, 142–143, 148–149, 161, 182–183, 193, 198–199, 202–203, 208, and 210–211.

© Daniel Dalton: p. 75.

© Christina Dannhausen-Brun: p. 185.

© Ellen Diamant: p. 201.

© Reg Down: p. 100.

© John Downs: p. 190.

© William Eberle: p. 115 (top).

© Don Emery: p. 43.

© Gary Ertter: p. 101.

© Captain William P. Gates: p. 87 (bottom).

© Harbortowne Marine: p. 62.

© Chip Henderson: pp. 134 and 162.

© Christopher Herbert: p. 76.

© Duncan Johnson: p. 200.

© Forest Johnson: pp. 4–5, 135, 150, 157, 160, 163, 166 (both), 167, 172–173, 178, 204–205, 214–215, and 216–217.

© Steven Lapkin: pp. 14–15 and 37.

© Jamie Lynn Laurent: p. 109.

© Aaron LeDonne: pp. 41, 45, 72–73, 92–93, 107, 112–113, 120–121, and 222.

© Carl Lovas: p. 102.

© Alex Lukash: pp. 164–165.

Courtesy of the Mariners' Museum: pp. 19, 23, 24 (both), 25, 28, 30, 31 (all), 32 (both), 33, 35 (both), 50, 51, 52, 53 (both), 56 (both), 57, 60 (all), 63 (both), 66–67, 110, and 224.

© George McInnis: p. 77.

© Charlie McMillen: pp. 12–13, 114, 221, and Nick Voulgaris jacket photo.

© Trent Mulloy: p. 179.

© Geoffrey Nesbit: p. 34.

© Courtesy of Ralph Peer: p. 124.

© Andrea Rakopoulos: p. 196.

© Jake Schnake/Matt Mason Photography: pp. 6–7 and 192.

© Edward Scott: p. 97.

© Joseph Signorelli: pp. 122–123.

© Ron Stevenson: p. 58.

© Charles Still: pp. 70, 71, and 118 (bottom).

© Jennifer Tee: pp. 144–145, 146, 152–153, 154–155, 158–159, 176–177, 180–181, 184, 206, 209, 218, and front cover.

© Daniel Teetor: pp. 16, 20, and 26–27.

© Scott Turnbull: p. 22.

© Wes Vandt: pp. 44, 54–55, 78, 80–81, and 91 (both).

© Nick Voulgaris: pp. 2–3, 10, 29, 36, 39, 40, 42, 46, 49, 59, 61, 64, 65, 68, 69, 74, 79 (both), 82, 83, 84, 85, 86, 87 (top), 90, 94, 95, 96, 99, 103, 108, 111, 116–117, 118 (top), 119, 125, 126–127, 128, 129, 188–189, 191, 207, 212–213, and 219.

© Bruce Weber: p. 9 and Ralph Lauren jacket photo.

© Mike Woodhouse: pp. 174–175.

Wecatchem, a 1948 Sportsman 25.

First published in the United States of America in 2018
Rizzoli International Publications, Inc.   •   300 Park Avenue South   •   New York, NY 10010   •   www.rizzoliusa.com

© 2018 CC Marine Brand Acquisition LLC   •   Foreword © 2018 Ralph Lauren

Associate Publisher: James Muschett   •   Text: Nick Voulgaris III   •   Project Editor: Candice Fehrman   •   Book Design: Susi Oberhelman

Chris ★ Craft

Crafted with the same passion and dedication as they were 144 years ago, Chris-Craft boats continue to speak to boat enthusiasts everywhere.
For more information, please visit www.chriscraft.com.

2018 2019 2020 2021 / 10 9 8 7 6 5 4 3 2 1

Printed in China   •   ISBN-13: 978-0-8478-6174-3   •   Library of Congress Catalog Control Number: 2017957453

PAGE 1: A young boy on the bow of a Chris-Craft Launch. PAGES 2–3: The legend of Chris-Craft continues today, as evidenced here by modern runabouts cruising alongside their historic counterparts on Lake Geneva, Wisconsin. PAGES 4–5: A Chris-Craft Corsair with its sleek, closed-bow design and overnight cabin. Chris-Craft returned this famous nameplate into production in 2002. PAGES 6–7: A fleet of contemporary and vintage Chris-Craft boats run on a still lake. PAGE 224: A company archive photo of a child aboard the bow of a Chris-Craft Runabout.